THE
LEADERSHIP
CODE OF CONDUCT

CULTURE CHANGE MADE SIMPLE

CAREY G. MACCONNELL

This book is dedicated to all the great people
I worked with at the Bartow Facility.

Contents

Introduction

What makes a good leader? Today there are thousands of books that give us the answer. Leadership books dissect the key traits and characteristics of effective leaders, how they understand their customers, and the ways in which they should serve their employees, organization and communities.

All too often people want a book, a website or an instructional list to give them the perfect definition of a successful leader, from how to look, how to act in specific situations, what to say and when, and with whom to associate. They want a full proof description of characteristics and behaviors to emulate. They want to follow the instructions so that successful leadership will just—happen.

Many renowned leadership book authors give us plenty of information and instructions. Take Peter Drucker, who has published over 20 books on this subject. I would never say that any of his theories are wrong; he is an extremely intelligent man who has observed, studied, dissected and interpreted every movement of a successful versus unsuccessful leaders.

Over the course of my career, it became apparent to me that effective leadership is not so complicated. Like many people, my work allowed me the opportunity to get to know a variety of unique individuals. One thing I learned is whether I was running analyses in a small back room in a laboratory or leading a major industrial production facility of 400 employees, when working with others there are always ways to act as a leader. There are ways to support a culture that can be embraced by all types of individuals, which creates one great place to work, and in turn produces undeniable fantastic results.

Leaders are the hinge that allows the doors to open in an organization. They need to create a culture that will breathe success. It's not one that is designed around red tape, a multitude of training sessions, or constant surveys, but rather by leaders who create and model a *Leadership Code of Conduct* (*LCC*) for their team, colleagues, customers and suppliers. The *LCC* provides a unified atmosphere for everyone in the workplace to interact in complementary ways. And once a culture has adapted to operate in these ways, success is only a matter of time.

So what is the *Leadership Code of Conduct*, and how does it differ from other traditional cultural approaches, trainings, seminars, or books on leadership?

> **It is simple.**
>
> **I repeat.**
>
> **It is simple.**

It is logical, and any person, no matter what level of responsibilities s/he has in an organization, the *LCC* is same.

That's right—it is no different for a president of a corporation or a laborer, for the Baby Boomers or Generation X employees. The Code does not discriminate. By following the *LCC*, you create a culture of success by leading everyone in how to interact.

The *Leadership Code of Conduct*

is a simple approach

that can be used worldwide

and will deliver success and happiness.

After all, they do go hand in hand,

don't they?

The Leadership Code of Conduct

4 Simple Steps

Truly Listen to People

Look for THE GOOD in People

Have Fun

Say Thank You

Take a moment to ask yourself:

Is it simple?

Does it make sense?

Can anyone at any level,
in any country, understand it?

Can I believe this?

Can I lead with these steps to
promote this culture?

Let's dive a little deeper…

1. **TRULY LISTEN TO PEOPLE**

   People want to be heard—It is a sign of respect.

2. **LOOK FOR THE GOOD IN PEOPLE**

   People do not wake up and say, "I am going to screw up today."

3. **HAVE FUN**

   You can take your job seriously with a smile on your face!

4. **SAY THANK YOU**

   EVERYONE wants to hear those words spoken with sincerity.

In my career, I served in leadership positions for over 30 years. During this time I developed a set of practices that promoted successful organizational culture, and led to attaining business process excellence to award winning levels. These practices comprise what I created as the *Leadership Code of Conduct*.

In this book you will learn how to apply the *Leadership Code of Conduct* in your workforce and everyday life. You'll learn how living all four of its simple concepts can change your organizational culture, and your results.

ONE
Truly Listen to People

Listening skills is a topic of many training classes, seminars, books, and even is an item on emotional intelligence surveys. How do we really listen to what people are saying? To make sure we're listening to people, we're commonly told things like: you must give others your undivided attention, which means shut down your computer, do not answer your phone, look them in the eye while they are talking, and do some type of nodding to make sure they think you are listening.

At work you may have also been asked to participate in an assessment of your personality as well as the personality of your team, so if there is a conflict you know what to do and how to act. I will almost guarantee that in one way or another the results of these kinds of assessments will include the feedback that our listening skills need to be improved. This means more training. But will more instruction give you the outcome you are looking for when it comes to a successful business, department, project, or life?

The truth is, it's not good enough to just follow instructions. Everyone you associate with needs to have the desire to learn the same techniques and listening skills. But does this happen as a result everyone listening to a facilitator for a couple hours? Do they walk out the training door with the ability to truly listen to what people are saying?

Learning to truly listen to people goes beyond this; it results in an *action* based on what you have heard. It may be to follow up on issues the person mentioned, to ask how the presentation went, or who won the baseball game. Truly listening to others also means delivering the actions in an authentic fashion. It establishes a culture of trust, respect and loyalty.

A story about a group of U.S. Air Force Academy Cadets tells us a lot about what it means to truly listen. A group of sophomore Cadets were busy with classes, drills, rules and regulations of the academy, and had the typical college student mentality of who was worth listening to and when.

It so happened that the Cadets had a special person in their midst and did not take the time to truly listen to what he was telling them. Who was this special person? The janitor of their dormitory. He was an older, quiet man and obviously closer to retirement than any of them! Any comments or advice he threw their way only received a polite nod before it rolled right over their heads. To the Cadets, he was a thing of the past and his value was minimized.

One day, an intelligent Cadet named Jim was doing some research for a paper on the Korean War when he read an article about a Mr. Evergreen. Mr. Evergreen single handedly, without concern for his own life, attacked enemy forces freeing his captured fellow soldiers. He was recognized by receiving the Metal of Honor.

Jim read the article one more time with a sense of caution and dismay. Was Mr. Evergreen our Mr. Evergreen—our janitor?

The next day Jim approached his fellow Cadets with the article and the theory that this person was one in the same. As his fellow Cadets were agreeing with him, there came Mr. Evergreen, coming around the corner with broom in hand. They all turned and stared at him with wide eyes.

Jim said, "Mr. Evergreen, I was reading this article—why didn't you tell us you received the Medal of Honor?" Mr. Evergreen just looked calmly at all the Cadets and replied, "To me I was just doing my duty—it was just another day."

After that day the Cadets and Mr. Evergreen, the janitor who held the Medal of Honor, became great friends. Advice, stories, instructions, and general talk became a daily occurrence. The Cadets learned so much from Mr. Evergreen over the next two years. Graduation day arrived and Jim's final and endearing comment to Mr. Evergreen was, "One of the many lessons you taught me over the years, Mr. Evergreen, was to truly listen to people, no matter who, where or what."

Let's take this lesson to your workplace. Take a few minutes to become an observer. The setting does not matter—it can be an industrial manufacturing plant setting or a call center. Over a short period of time you will be able to identify "unspoken" leaders of teams. How do you know that they are the unspoken leaders? How do they get this unofficial title? Because people go to them to hold a discussion, to ask their opinion, and to them about the greatest baseball play their son accomplished the night before in little league. It may appear that they are spending way too much time socializing, but is that what they are really doing?

What they are really doing is listening to all, with no bias and a totally transparent face to each and every person with whom they work. They are the listeners, the ones that take the time out of their busy schedule to stop and truly listen to what folks are saying.

We know they are listening well. Why? Because people return. People will not return to you if you are not truly listening to them.

And a company where people listen to each other means high employee engagement, which results in trust and respect for each other. That's a culture we all want to be part of.

A team development meeting I was once in makes an even further point about listening. A group of high level professionals were having a difficult time working together, so they set up a structured set of team development sessions. In the first session, they were asked strategic questions to get people to open up. It moved slowly, which was understandable, given it was their very first session.

Interestingly, the conversation turned away from their team, and turned to issues related to others outside of their team, such as they ways in which they (not them) did not understand, they needed more education, they were misinterpreting decisions.

Then one individual, with a sense of urgency, as if it was an epiphany says, "What our problem is—is we do not listen. Our customers are telling us one thing but we are interpreting it in *our way* in *our time*—we're just not listening."

If the leadership team was not truly listening to their customers, how well were they listening to each other? Obviously not very well, because they needed a team building session to come together. They needed to start with themselves.

To truly listen to people, we need to listen closely enough so we can take an immediate action that tells others we were paying attention to them and what they were saying.

Think about times when you felt confident you were being heard—was there an action that resulted? I bet there was.

Two
Look for the Good in People

Look for the good in people— what a powerful phrase. People do not wake up in the morning and say they want to come to work to screw up! People really do want to do a great job and want to be recognized for it.

Think about yourself when you held various levels of responsibility, when people believed in you and your abilities. You worked harder to ensure a successful outcome not just for yourself but for your boss, your colleagues and your organization, right?

Here is a story about what can happen when we "look for the good in people." I was working in a large industrial manufacturing plant setting with 400 employees, and had just been promoted to superintendent. I was in my mid-thirties at the time. My promotion was the first time that a woman held this position, and many employees had questioned this decision when it was made.

The plant had been around for years and in the family generations. Grandfathers, fathers and sons all worked in the same location. The plant operated 24 hours a day, seven days a week, 365 days a year. People at the plant would say that they spent more of their waking hours with the people at work with than their own families.

One Thursday afternoon about 2:30 p.m., about one hour before shift change I had an encounter with one of my employees named Simon. He had been a well-respected, seasoned shift supervisor for 40 years. We met in the dim hallway that led to the plant's maintenance shop, and stood eye to eye when the conversation began. He started spouting out all the issues that plant was currently having that afternoon, from potential emergency shut downs to poor product quality due to mechanical failures. He must have brought up about five that in his opinion needed an immediate action. Time was a factor because the majority of the day mechanics were winding down and getting ready to head home for the day.

Without even a breath, and with a sense of urgency in his voice, he asked me, "What do you want to do, shut down? What do you want to repair? When and how?"

Without much hesitation I looked directly at Simon and replied, "Can I ask you a question before I answer your questions?" Of course he agreed, and looked surprised when I asked him this question: "Let's pretend it was three in the morning on a Saturday and you were the supervisor on duty—what would you do?" He was a bit taken aback at first, then confidently gave an answer that indicated he knew exactly what would need to be done.

Then I simply stated, "It seems to me that you already know what needs to be done, so why are you asking me? You are quite capable. All I ask is that you keep me informed of your decisions."

His eyes grew wide, and you could see a sense of pride come over his face. He immediately interpreted what I had really told him: he was good at what he does and I had confidence in his abilities. He turned around and took care of the matter.

Simon became one of my number one supporters, all because I *looked for the good* in him and his abilities and showcased it by demonstrating confidence in him.

And by the way, the plant continued to improve until it was breaking all kinds of records!

When people recognize the positive in others it will result in a series of positive behaviors. Here are tips to keep your focus on looking for the good:

- In your workplace, avoid saying "can't," "don't" and "unacceptable" to employees. They will be more positive and open about listening to potential changes that will help reach goals.

- High stress situations can lead to negativity, which does not help the sincerity of looking for the good in people. If you are in a challenging situation and feel a negative cloud coming over you, take a quick walk. New surroundings, even for a few minutes before addressing colleagues can change your attitude.

- At home, minimize the amount of news you watch on television or read on the web. Much of it has a tendency to draw the negative and impact your outlook.

- Smile while driving—to work, to the store, to pick up your kids at school. It is a proven fact that the act of smiling will send the correct neurons to your brain resulting in a positive behavior.

Authors Joseph Granny, Kerry Patterson, David Mayfield and Ron McMillan tell a great story in their book, *Influencer*, which captures the essence of looking for the good in people. This particular story is powerful and is a great example of how anyone, with any background, at any level of responsibility, can look for the positive in others, and support them to get great results not just for themselves but for all individuals.

The story is about a doctor who over the course of her career focused on finding the causes of and solutions to difficult behavioral problems. She contends that it is not emotions or even values, but looking for the good behavior in others is what will permanently change people's behaviors.

The doctor worked with over 14,000 criminals. One of her behavioral approaches was to require each person to take responsibility for someone else's success. In order to make this happen, one person had to focus on and believe that the other could complete and sustain the required task or assigned job, which would result in a positive outcome for both individuals.

Think about this, and apply this thought to your situation. Isn't it a leader's responsibility to ensure success? Both for people and the company? If you look for the good in people, do you think that would assist in changing their behavior? The doctor thought so, as did over 97 percent of the people that went through her sponsored by the Delancey Street Foundation.

Years ago I heard another story that fits the *LCC* extremely well. Here is the person's story:

> *It was a dark, rather gloomy day in the city of Boston. Clouds had been hovering for days, and there were periodic downpours of rain that*

soaked everyone. The gloomy days just added to a gloomy atmosphere at work. Things were not going as planned, people were on edge, and tempers were rising.

The past couple days all I really wanted to do was get on the subway and sit quietly for my 30 minute ride, go home to my own sanctuary and not worry about business issues—at least not until tomorrow. That day, I got on the subway a little later than normal with a splitting headache.

At the first stop I was introduced to little Fred and Susie. Fred looked like he was about four or five years old and Susie looked a little older, about seven or eight. Their father looked like a deadbeat dad. He pushed them on the train and sat down in the corner, expressionless. Fred and Susie were pretty wound up; in sibling fashion they pushed each other around, told on each other and became uncontrollable in this cramped public setting. I was getting extremely irritated with the entire situation, and with their dad, who was doing nothing.

Finally, after 10 minutes of putting up with this, with my stress level reaching a high, I looked at their dad and said, "Your kids are pretty disruptive today—can you do something about it?"

He looked up rather surprised, but when his eyes contacted mine, they looked sad. There was even a glossy film over them. He replied in a very quiet tone, "I am sorry if they are bothering you, I usually do not allow them to misbehave. You see we just left the hospital. Their mother has died and I do not know what to do.

I do not know how to talk to them and explain that she is not coming back. They just have so much energy right now, but I do not. I really apologize for not addressing their behavior."

Then he called his children over and told them to sit quietly next to him until they reached their stop. They actually did exactly what he told them. The three sat there as I stared in disbelief.

Did having a bad day give me the right to assume that this man was a "dead beat dad?" I learned instead I could choose to focus on him in a positive way and offer a supportive question like, "Hello, you look distraught today, or that you might not be feeling well. I noticed your children are pretty excitable—what can I do to help settle them down?"

The moral of the story: Before jumping to conclusions that things are negative, bad, or just plain terrible, learn to look at situations from a positive side. Then you can approach and deal with them in an atmosphere that is willing to accept change, decisions, and actions with welcome arms. It will create a culture of positive thinking.

Positive thoughts will—I assure you—result in great things!

THREE
Have Fun

Have fun. This is simple, but believe it or not, for a lot of people it can be very difficult. Why? Because they believe that in order to be taken seriously you have to *be* serious and impersonal. On the contrary, having fun will bring you closer together with your team and create relationships with fantastic communication!

Communication means collaboration, which is a characteristic of a successful organization. How many of us have participated in a team building exercise, and the reason why we were invited was to improve the cohesiveness of the team? Did it work? What happened afterwards—was the cohesiveness sustainable?

The *Leadership Code of Conduct* focuses on having fun because you can be serious about your job with a smile on your face. Body language research tells us that when you deliver a message, the expression on your face tells 80 percent of the message. So if you can deliver a message, even a difficult one, in a positive way, think of the response you will receive.

Here is a case in point. At the same the industrial manufacturing plant site I described earlier, I was now the general manager, and each weekday morning I met with my superintendents to discuss opportunities, problems, compliance opportunities, downtime, production numbers, and safety issues. These discussions could be difficult when operations were not achieving desired results.

I had a philosophy that ensured my superintendents left these meetings with smile on their faces, as they headed out to attack the issues of the day—good and bad. I developed a few traditions that took place at these meetings. First, I always started on a positive note, enthusiastically wishing everyone a "Good Morning!"

Then I briefly discussed the "meaning" of the day, such as a specific holiday in another country, or a special "day" declared by a card manufacturer. All birthdays of folks around the table were also always recognized.

Then everyone had their opportunity to speak about the issues of the day. Once this took place it was time for my tradition of reading a quote for the day. Humorous or philosophical, everyone grew to expect my quote of the day.

Next and most important was the "fun" portion. It would only take five to seven minutes and was designed to ensure that when they left to address potential difficult situations, they did not meet their employees with a negative, irritated look on their faces. I wanted them to be able to greet their employees with a positive, yet straightforward attitude. Fun actions included things like riddles (three at a time), a word game call Mad Gab, or three (clean) jokes from a joke book. Even the corniest jokes would catch a laugh.

I knew that a big key to having fun in a workplace meant everyone participates, including me. I made sure I was always right in the middle of the action, from singing to the employee of the month to dressing up as Mrs. Santa Claus during the holidays. I embodied the idea that having fun is not something you assign to other people; it's something you fully engage in yourself.

We all know how the workplace can be very stressful. Laughter is a key to reducing stress. This is based on medical fact. Stress enters other areas of our lives as well. We each have our own way of dealing with it. What is a powerful stress reducer for us all? It's laughter—something that is far more contagious than any cough, sniffle or sneeze!

Shared laughter binds people together, increases happiness and grows trust. Humor and laughter can physically strengthen your immune system, boost energy, and diminish pain. It releases endorphins, a good body chemical that promotes a sense of well-being and stabilized blood pressure.

In a word, laughter is healthy!

Just as there is power in laughter, there is power in a smile. It's common knowledge that part of training for a successful sales person is to smile. They learn to smile when making calls to set appointments, and smile while negotiating prices. More sales are made when people smile.

When in sales or any other role, a smile shows you are happy. It carries through in your speech, posture, and words. It shows you are enjoying yourself and having fun.

Here's the simple formula:
Fun + Smiles = Smart Decisions!

FOUR
Say Thank You

How hard is it to say thank you? Feedback on many surveys indicates it is very hard. Yet surveys also tell us that recognition is one of the top three areas that are important to employees. There are seminars, books, videos on the different way to recognize people. There are different ways to recognize: formal, informal, monetary, and even things like hand-written notes. One thing is certain; the recognition has to be given in a sincere, authentic fashion. People can see right through a fake. It is like looking through a glass window!

How is authentic defined? It means that you understand the effort that was taken to accomplish the task and can recognize it appropriately. It has to be personal. Making it personal means showing your gratitude in the most meaningful way in the eyes of the receiver.

Here is how I practiced this part of the *Leadership Code of Conduct*. Many industrial manufacturing plants strive to grow a safe culture, meaning keeping people from harm of any sort. The common practice is to set a safety goal to keep a common focus for a united outcome. Once a plant facility has reached the predetermined safety goal, recognition of that achievement is expected.

A monetary or a "nice" gift is a usual choice. These are very thoughtful and easy to purchase and distribute, especially for larger operations. Gifts are appreciated, but the question is—how personable was it? Was it enough to impress that a safety culture comprised of zero incidents was the direction the company strived to achieve?

In this case, I did not believe that only a gift sent the importance of the safety message to my employees. To send this message, I wrote a personal, handed-written congratulations note for every one of my 400 employees. I did not assign this to my administrative assistant—I personally wrote all of these notes.

It was not the actual gift or even the notes themselves, but the personal time and effort that I took with each note that showed the authentic appreciation for reaching the safety milestone. Authentic thank yous mean you have put some time and thought into how and what you say.

In today's times, people expect more thank yous. Why? Think about it—every day we have immediate feedback on how we are doing. We receive direct and indirect thank yous from all kinds of sources—through Facebook, Twitter, texting, surfing the Internet, even computer games. We use Google to search for information, and we get immediate results, often in seconds.

Folks today do not want to wait until the end of a six month project to start receiving recognition. They want to hear something immediate and continuous. So not only do we need to thank and recognize people in a sincere and authentic fashion, we need to do it very soon after we get the results that deserve recognition. This is a powerful part of the *LCC*.

Summing It All Up

When the *Leadership Code of Conduct* is embraced by all leaders, and they model the idea that everyone at some point is a leader, an organization will have all the characteristics for success.

The result will be engagement, customer loyalty, community embracement and of course, positive financial returns. The *LCC* will ignite trust, collaboration, connectivity, and unity.

To sum it up:

Everyone is significant.

Everyone is a leader.

When everyone practices the simple concepts

in the *Leadership Code of Conduct*

Everyone can drive cultural change.

How do you embrace the LCC?

First and foremost, you must believe in this approach. If you cannot "walk the talk" of the *Leadership Code of*

Conduct, go back and read a book, or attend a seminar—it will help, but it is not the *Code*!

Believe it

then

Lead with it

and

Live it!

In your workplace, make posters, print business cards, and do creative, tangible things to recognize the values of the *LCC*. Adherence should be (well, almost) just as powerful as the military code.

Remember, if all people accept it, if it becomes the organizational culture, the backbone of your organization, there is nothing that cannot be accomplished!

So, back to the questions
from the beginning...

Is it simple?

Does it make sense?

Can anyone at any level,
in any country, understand it?

Can I believe this?

And the last question is: Can I lead an organization to embrace this culture?

As a leader, success is in your hands.

Employing the *Leadership Code of Conduct* is simply your choice!

The Leadership Code of Conduct

Truly Listen to People

Look for the Good in People

Have Fun

Say Thank You!

About Carey MacConnell

Carey MacConnell has been in organizational leadership positions for over 30 years. She started her career working in the back room of an analytical laboratory as an individual contributor and rose to successfully managing an industrial manufacturing facility of over 400 employees.

She successfully led business process excellence to award winning levels, and changed company culture to embrace the *Leadership Code of Conduct*, which created success for many of her colleagues, financial success for organizations she worked for, and instilled customer loyalty, safety, effective production and employee engagement.

Carey is passionate about ensuring everyone she works with at all levels of responsibility have the opportunity to shine. She is a master at coaching for success, and believes that success is surrounding yourself with intelligent, driven people, all leading towards an organization's cultural revolution.

www.ingramcontent.com/pod-product-compliance
Lightning Source LLC
Chambersburg PA
CBHW070722210326
41520CB00016B/4427

9 7 8 0 6 1 5 8 8 2 0 3 1